W9-BGJ-756

First Biographies
Charles M. Schulz

by Cheryl Carlson

Consulting Editor: Gail Saunders-Smith, PhD

Capstone
press

Mankato, Minnesota

Pebble Books are published by Capstone Press,
151 Good Counsel Drive, P.O. Box 669, Mankato, Minnesota 56002.
www.capstonepress.com

1 2 3 4 5 6 10 09 08 07 06 05

Library of Congress Cataloging-in-Publication Data
Carlson, Cheryl.
   Charles M. Schulz/by Cheryl Carlson
   p. cm.—(First biographies)
   Includes bibliographical references and index.
   ISBN 0-7368-3638-1 (hardcover)
   1. Schulz, Charles M.—Juvenile literature. 2. Cartoonists—United States—
Biography—Juvenile literature. I. Title. II. Series: First biographies (Mankato, Minn.)
PN6727.S3Z625 2005
741.5'092—dc22   2004011973

Summary: Simple text and photographs present the life of Charles M. Schulz.

Note to Parents and Teachers

The First Biographies set supports national history standards for
units on people and culture. This book describes and illustrates the
life of Charles M. Schulz. The images support early readers in
understanding the text. The repetition of words and phrases helps
early readers learn new words. This book also introduces early
readers to subject-specific vocabulary words, which are defined in
the Glossary section. Early readers may need assistance to read
some words and to use the Table of Contents, Glossary, Read More,
Internet Sites, and Index sections of the book.

Table of Contents

Time Line

1922
born

Early Years

Charles M. Schulz was born in 1922 in Minnesota. Charles was an only child. He was a good student.

Time Line

1922
born

Drawing

Charles loved to draw.
He drew a picture
of his dog, Spike.
The cartoon of Spike
was printed in
a newspaper in 1937.

Time Line

1922
born

1943
joins army

Charles graduated from
high school in 1940.
He drew cartoons
and comic strips for fun.
In 1943, he joined
the army.

Time Line

1922
born

1943
joins army

In the late 1940s,
Charles was an art school
teacher in Minnesota.
He helped other people
learn how to draw.

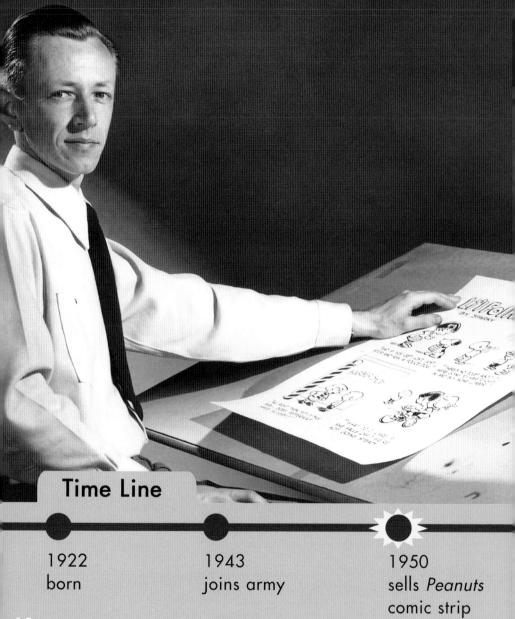

Time Line

1922
born

1943
joins army

1950
sells *Peanuts*
comic strip

Peanuts

Charles sold a comic strip in 1950. The publisher named it *Peanuts*. People read *Peanuts* in the newspaper.

Time Line

1922	1943	1950
born	joins army	sells *Peanuts* comic strip

Peanuts was about
a boy named Charlie Brown.
Charlie Brown had
a dog named Snoopy.
Peanuts became famous.

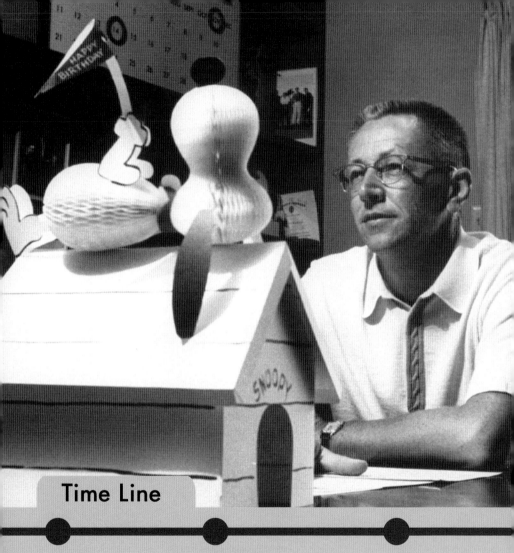

Time Line

1922
born

1943
joins army

1950
sells *Peanuts*
comic strip

Charles moved to California with his wife and five children in 1958.
In 1965, a *Peanuts* cartoon was on TV for the first time.

 Charles sitting in his studio

1965
Peanuts appears
on TV

Time Line

1922
born

1943
joins army

1950
sells *Peanuts*
comic strip

Awards

People around the world read *Peanuts* in newspapers. Charles won many awards for his work. He was given a Hollywood Star in 1996.

1965
Peanuts appears
on TV

1996
receives
Hollywood Star

Time Line

1922
born

1943
joins army

1950
sells *Peanuts*
comic strip

Remembering Charles

Charles died in 2000. Today, people still remember Charles and his *Peanuts* characters. Some people have parades to honor him.

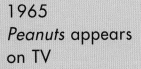

1965
Peanuts appears
on TV

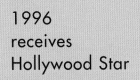

1996
receives
Hollywood Star

2000
dies

Glossary

cartoon—a funny drawing

character—one of the people in a story, book, movie, or play; Charles sometimes added new characters to *Peanuts*.

comic strip—a story told using panels of cartoons; many newspapers print comic strips.

publisher—a person or group that makes books, newspapers, and other printed items for people to read

Read More

Klingel, Cynthia Fitterer, and Robert B. Noyed.
Charles Schulz: A Level Two Reader. Chanhassen,
Minn.: Child's World, 2002.

Marvis, Barbara J. *Charles Schulz.* A Robbie Reader.
Hockessin, Del.: Mitchell Lane, 2005.

Woods, Mae. *Charles Schulz.* Children's Authors.
Edina, Minn.: Abdo, 2002.

Internet Sites

FactHound offers a safe, fun way to find Internet sites
related to this book. All of the sites on FactHound
have been researched by our staff.

Here's how:

1. Visit *www.facthound.com*

2. Type in this special code **0736836381** for
   age-appropriate sites. Or enter a search word
   related to this book for a more general search.

3. Click on the **Fetch It** button.

FactHound will fetch the best sites for you!

Index

Word Count: 186
Grade: 1
Early-Intervention Level: 15

Editorial Credits
Sarah L. Schuette, editor; Heather Kindseth, set designer; Patrick D. Dentinger, book
    designer; Kelly Garvin, photo researcher; Scott Thoms, photo editor

Photo Credits
Aurora/Jose Azel, 1, 14
Charles M. Schulz Museum, 4, 6, 8, 10, 12, 18
Corbis/Reuters, cover
Getty Images/Time Life Pictures/Nat Farbman, 16
Zuma Press/P. J. Heller, 20